The Edge of Listening

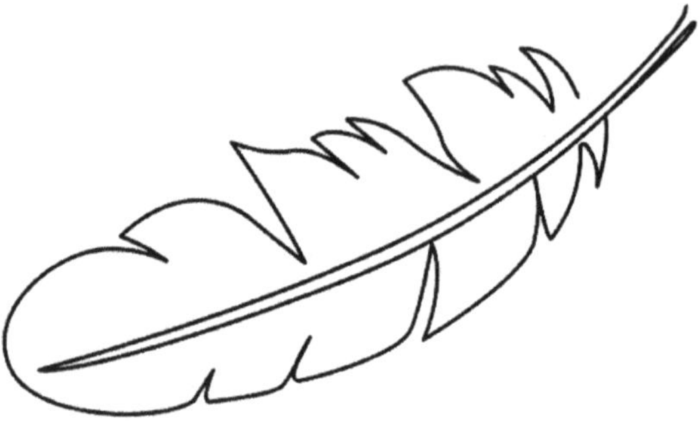

The Edge of Listening

Poems of Silence, Longing, and Return

by Debashis Dey

First published in India in 2025
ISBN: 978-93-343-2646-8
Published by: Little Cloud Co

Cover design by Debashis Dey
Interior illustrations by Debashis Dey & Others
Author Website: www.debashisdey.com

For those who wait in silence

Acknowledgements

To the drifting clouds, the autumn leaves, the silvery stream in moonlight. To the wind that carried my questions into the trees. To those whose silence held more truth than speech. To every moment that waited for me to listen—and to the ones who unknowingly inspired a line or held space for a poem to arrive.

A Note to The Reader

There was a time I wasn't sure if I would ever share these poems. Not because they were unfinished, but because they felt too quiet—like whispers only meant for me.

Each poem in this collection holds a thread of silence I have lived with: moments too fragile to speak of, memories I carried like shadows, and feelings I could never quite explain aloud. Writing them was not an act of ambition, but of listening—listening to the spaces between things, the tremble of wind through leaves, the voice that echoes long after someone has gone.

I don't claim to be a poet in any formal sense. I have no technique to boast of, no academy to lean on. Only the weight of stillness, and the instinct to shape that stillness into words.

Some of these poems arrived whole, like rain. Others came in fragments, like driftwood. They were never meant to impress, only to express—what could not be held in thought alone.

If any of these verses speak to something you've quietly carried, then I'll know they've done their work.

And for that, I'll be grateful.

—Debashis

What Readers Are Saying

Silence, not as the absence of sound, but as the presence of quiet introspection, pervades these gentle, reflective poems. Soft as gossamer, the words weave dreamlike images of the sublime and mysterious beauty of Nature, of a woman's slender wrist adorned with a green bangle, and of small reminders of a former lover. Elegant line drawings beautifully complement this collection of delicate musings on the passing of time, on desire and loss, and on healing.

—Kalpana Shenoi,
Former Lecturer in English, Peter Symonds College of Winchester

Debashis Dey's poetry uses vivid and evocative language and invites readers to inhale the essence of love and self- discovery! His poetry is influenced by the rhythms of speech!

—Gopal Lahiri
Award winning poet, editor, and translator.

Silence, nature, and emotion echo through this collection in a dream-like cadence. There is a soft hush in these lines, an underlying music that keeps ringing beyond the covers. Divided in sections, united by the string of the poet's intense artistic eye, this book surely announces the arrival of a strong voice who knows his canvas.

—Raja Chakraborty
Poet

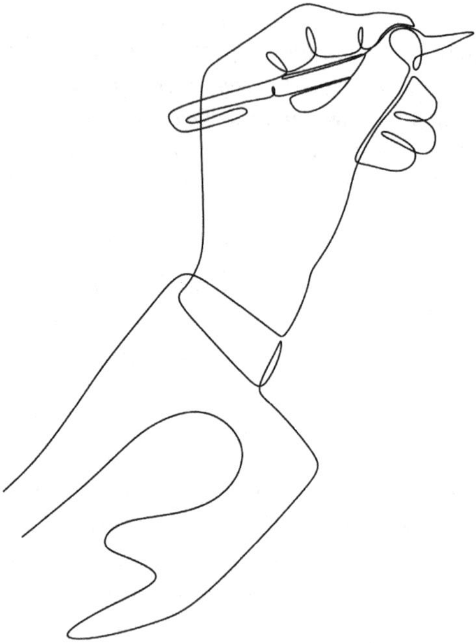

Table of Contents

III. Nude And Other Lies

IV. Ways of Not Arriving

V. Nocturne of The Forgotten

VI. Interlude Before the Epilogue

VII. Before the Light Returns

Epilogue

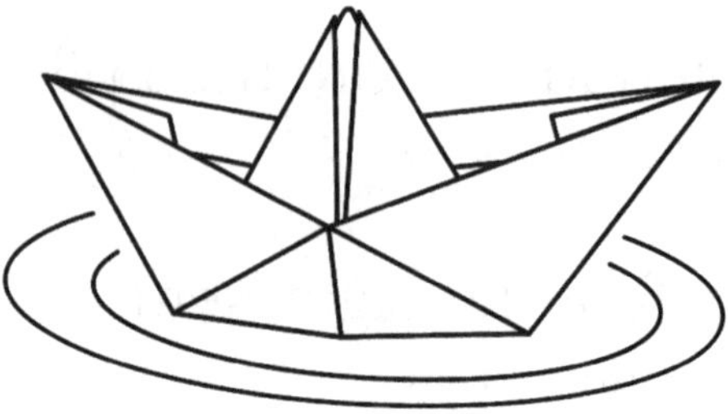

Prologue

The Edge of Listening

There are places
where silence isn't absence;
it's presence,
retaining the shape
of what the world neglected to say.
The sea,
the mountain,
and the forest
all listen
in their own ancient way,
not with ears
but with memories.
These are the lines
we cross without knowing it –
The wind turns into words,
the stone becomes into scripture,
and the leaves remember
what we haven't yet learnt to feel.
Stand here,
at the edge of listening.
Let the world be quiet
and become
what you hear.

I. What the Wind Remembers

"It moves through fields of withered grain,
stirs the quiet in hollow trees—
the wind remembers
what moss keeps secret
and rivers fail to say."

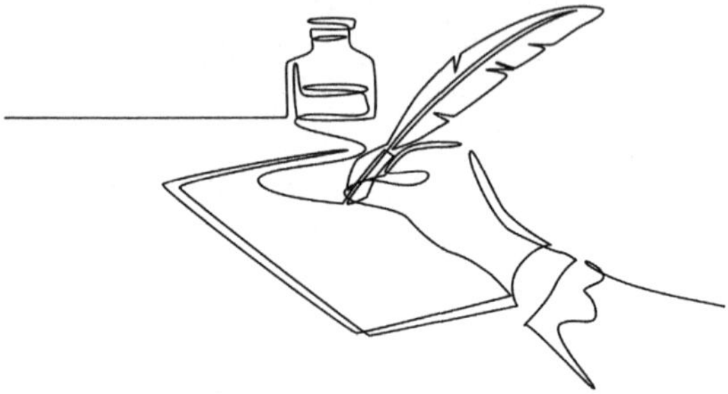

Where Silence Writes

I watch silence
unfurl in ripples—
across the blue skin of water,
each wave a breath
held by the world.

I watch it drift—
a billion stars
moving across the sky
in a calm procession,
their beauty beyond melody.

The crescent moon
hovers on a calm sea,
its silver lip caressing
the dark edge of the mon-
soon.

The river flows
like a silver line
through a valley
that is dreaming.

I watch the peaks—
snow-capped and listening—
soften into silence,
their thawing hearts
blessing the waiting falls.

I watch silence touch
each unopened bud—
a promise whispered
in the language of spring.

And I watch it write
across the earth—
poetry without ink,
without end.
A language, that never dies.

The Silence of Stone

Silent they stand—
the mountains—
whispering all that is.
Every ridge whispers
a line carved by the breeze,
every crevice
a sigh suspended
since time began.

I rest at their feet,
a seeker of quietude,
looking up
at their serene sanctuary.
Their pause is not void—
it is rich,
laden with the gravity
of unspoken truths.

Veils of mist entwine,
like memories of incense lost,
while pines murmur softly,
in tongues
that only the birds remember.
Fossils rest in the creases—
pieces of tales
sandwiched between strata of rock,
moments layered upon moments,
remembrance turned to dust.

The air is lighter
in this realm,
yet heavy with whispers—
the tread of holy men,
the clatter of age-old rhythms,
a soothing song
once offered to celestial bodies
now dimmed.
A hawk soars in the sky,
not as a predator—
but as an observer.

Even the sun glides gently here,
as if to hush
what dreams beneath the frost.
In silence,
I seek not for replies.
I find no solace in prayer.
I only listen—
to the stillness
between the tumbling stones,
to the hush that collects
like a gentle blanket
on the spirit.

The mountains—
do not move
They remain steadfast.
They hold onto
the echoes of the past.
And in their recalling,
I start to lose
all but the essence of breath.

The Forest Remembers

The forest does not forget.
It remembers everything—
the stir of ancient winds,
the weight of moss-covered sorrow,
the wild pulse
of something older than names.

I walk where light filters
like breath through cathedral leaves,
where vines twist
in slow, deliberate prayers
around trunks that hold
the memory of rain.

There is a scent here—
damp, green, and primitive.
The fragrance of beginnings,
of bark and spore,
of the earth dreaming itself
into form again.

Leaves stir
not with welcome,
but with recognition.
The air is thick with knowing.
Even the silence
has age rings here,
layered in tranquility,
layered in shadow.

A fox glides past—
its presence more suggestion than sight.
Somewhere,
a bird sings a single note,
and everything stills—
as if the forest, too,
is remembering a long-lost word
it buried beneath its roots.

I reach the clearing
where light pools like forgotten gold
at the feet of watching trees.
Nothing shouts.
Even the wind moves reverently.
The branches arch above me,
not in shade—
but benediction.

I sit among roots
that breathe like slow hearts,
my thoughts falling away
like dried leaves.
And I listen—
to the stillness
between wingbeats,
to the whisper
beneath bark,
to the murmur
in my blood
that does not belong to me.

This is no wilderness—
this is a memory
older than the sky,

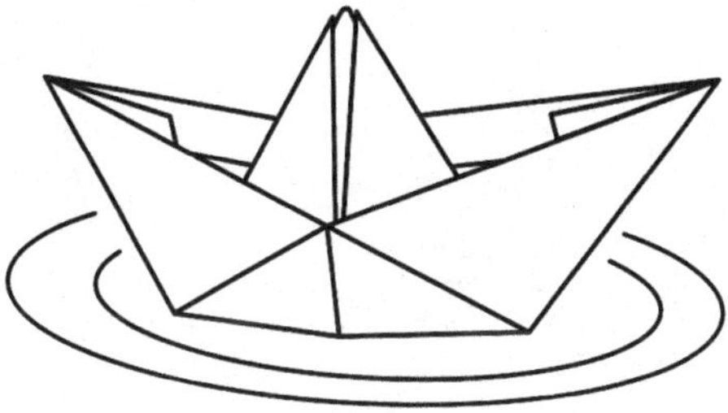

And somewhere,
beyond the hush of stone
and the pull of the tide,
the forest joins them—
in the great, quiet listening
that holds us all.

Through The Quiet of You
– Some journeys are taken in silence.

Maybe for you —
I taste the auburn lull of autumn,
where leaves fall like forgotten names,
and cloud-puffs vanish
on southern winds,
carrying my thoughts
into their forgetting.

I watch the stars burn out in silence,
a foolish smile blooming
through sleepless dark.
I follow their echo —
light that died a thousand years ago,
and still dares to shine.

I walk the road alone,
not for the end,
but for the pause between steps.
Not to arrive,
but to remember—
how breath once held your name,
how solitude folded sweetly beneath my ribs.

Maybe for you —
I turn away,
choosing the hidden trail
where the world forgets to follow,
where longing can live
and not be silenced,
and the trees keep secrets
only dusk can hear.

Maybe for you —
I learn to love
what vanishes slowly,
what waits without asking,
what moves like prayer
through the quiet of you.

Where The Sky Whispers

At the horizon,
where the sky bows gently
to share tender murmurs
with the eager sea,
I sit—
resting upon a weathered stone,
observing ripples gleam
like whispers exchanged
from wave to wave.

The light shifts gently,
a melody of colors—
purple ash, scorched pink,
soft gold mingling with azure.
Clouds wander like lost missives
never delivered,
twisting at the fringes
with thoughts unvoiced.

In tranquil moments,
I attune to whispers,
to harmonies once submerged,
now gently ascending
upon a zephyr
that recognises my essence
yet speaks it only in reverberations.

Underneath these timeless stones,
secret chambers resonate
with echoes I've yet to claim—
glimmers of a flame
once kindled
in the depths of my heart.
And still I gaze
as the moonlight fractures
into countless silver blossoms,
each one floating
on the crest of a crescent wave,
swaying gently toward eternity.

A vessel emerges—
remote, ethereal,
its canvas laden with fog,
constellations ensnared in its lines
its sails heavy with mist,
stars tangled in its rigging.
It does not move.
Or perhaps it only moves
for those who've given up
on destinations.

I wonder
if it carries old songs,
or letters in bottles
from those
who once waited here too.
Maybe it is my grief
sailing past me again
in another form.

The stars blink—
not as guideposts,
but as memories.
Some are still burning.
Some are long dead,
their light only now
reaching me.
The sea,
eternally in conversation
with the sky,
never asks questions,
never offers answers—
only rhythm.

And I,
a quiet witness,
remain seated
on this ancient rock,
with thoughts I do not speak,
and pain I do not name.

Not waiting for someone.
Not even for time.
Just watching the sky
fall in love with the sea
again and again
and again.

Sometimes, The River

At times...
the river beckons me—
to stroll alongside her
where the dew-kissed grass
and the polished stones
gleam with the whispers of stars
collected in quietude
on nights
devoid of moonlight.

She hums in ripples,
a low murmur
that knows my name,
carrying old songs
and the scent
of rain-washed soil.

And at times...
she does not murmur—
she dances.
Her curves gleam
like the silhouette of a muse
just beyond grasp,
each contour whispering
of treasures ahead:
the sparkle of joy,
the pang of desire.

She bends in brilliance,
bubbled and shining,
nudging gentle curves
against the very essence of time—
She calls me to drift—
not to paddle,
just to surrender.
“Allow the form to float,” she murmurs,
“and I shall bear the spirit.”

At times…
she remains silent—
merely urging me to believe,
to shut my eyes,
and surrender
to the endless, shimmering line
that connects all existence
to the boundless joy
that lingers
just around the corner.

And thus I drift,
unaware of my path—
only that bliss beckons
in fields uncharted,
where the heavens kiss the sea,
and all that was forsaken.

Drift Beyond

- Among the ruins of unsaid things

When
the morning's soft light
settles lightly on your skin
when the sun, strung on birdsong,
spills blue across the far sky,
drift away —

in the wandering, trembling scribbles
of my broken pages,
drift away.

And
when heavy clouds
nest inside your eyes,
they belong —
like a secret kept too long.
When morning's breath,
woven with old sorrow,
stirs half-awake dreams,
weave through the shadows —
in the earth's damp, forgotten music,
drift away.

When
the sun, weary with its return,
sinks colors into the river's skin,
melt into the dream —
in the blurred sketches
of unsung songs,
fade with the mist.

When
the stars, wet with sleep,
pause on the frozen hem of clouds,
then,
in the quiet fever of my words,
let desire mislead you—
through the unseen alleys of my ache,
drift away.

The Quiet Will Carry You

-for the space between sorrow and light

You don't need to explain
the ache to the trees.
They've braved
a thousand storms,
shed leaves
without apology.
You don't need to name
the sorrow to the river.
It moves around stone,
not through it—
and still finds
its own reflection.
You don't need to heal
all at once.
Just sit where
the light drips in.
The silence will hold you.
The quiet will carry you.

Before The Mist Rises

When the morning drips
through the tangled breath of trees,
and the bustle of rain carries
the weight of forgotten sorrows,
woven into the trembling of mist-laden leaves…

When the sun, weary and returning,
scatters broken gold
across the sleeping roots,
spilling light
like letters buried in the loam...

When the clouds drift low,
veiling the weary eyes of ancient trees,
blinking softly
through the shivering shadows...

In those moments, my friend,
try and find your way —
through the echoes of rain-slicked songs,
through verses etched
along the gnarled spines of old bark,
through thoughts paved
with soaked roots and patient stones,
winding into the secret heart of the woods.

Try and find your way —
before the mist rises,
and the forest forgets you.

Everything Moves

As the leaf falls—
silently,
floating
on the gentle breath
of dawn.
As the grass bows low
to let the dew drop go.
As the mist rises
in shamanic trance—
Nothing—
yet everything
moves.

This Is the Hour When Silence Breathes

Now the night is silent—
and silence,
with darkness curled around its fingers,
spreads like a quiet empire.
Still, somewhere,
bubbles rise—
small sounds
surfacing
on forgotten streets.
They drift
through alleys and footpaths,
curling into cracks,
nestling in corners—
in pores,
in roots,
in veins and ribs and whispered breath.

The lamppost stands—
tall, blind,
casting light on others
but never seeing
its own reflection
beneath a thousand passing feet.

Not all sounds
are meant to be heard.
Some hide
behind the fuss of rain.
Some curl
into the folds of grief,
or dissolve
in silent defiance.
A few flicker
in the sheen of tired eyes.
A few remain unnamed,
circling like ghosts
in the space before dawn.
And now,
in this midnight hour,
the echoes of those scattered words
will stay—
not lost,
just resting quietly
in the pages of my notebook.

II. Where the Heart Waits

"Where the heart waits,
time drifts in quiet spirals—
love lingers in the folds of absence,
and memory gathers
like dusk in an empty room."

The Confluence

I saw her in the crowd, moving ahead
with confident strides, braving the summer heat,
hair flowing–framing her face.
And then she looked up–

As if she had felt my gaze… and I paused–
or perhaps the universe did.
That wordless moment brimmed with words
unspoken. Eyes met, and silence reigned.

Then, as if by some quiet orchestration,
a few things happened in swift succession:
A part of me broke away from myself–
the part that writes each night,
as if to a parallel world
where spring is eternal and untouched.

One man spoke, and both laughed,
drifting hand in hand to a coffee shop.
Now he will read her a few tired verses–
and perhaps, seek a night wrapped in passing warmth.

Another leaned in close, whispering words
I could almost recite–the ones
that brought a blush to her cheek.
He will ask her to pose, to undress,
to be framed in brushstrokes and candlelight.

A third stood across from her at the signal,
offering nothing but presence–
no lines, no plans, no clever approach–
just the stillness of someone
willing to walk beside her,
wordless, through any season.

And I–
I stand at the confluence of these imagined paths,
unsure which one to follow,
each leading to paths unknown
and maybe, just maybe,
to something beautifully unknown.

Wings For My Words
-Carry what I cannot hold.

Poetry, you go —
climb to the peak,
touch the untouched snow,
and sit there a while,
watching the wide sky breathe.

Place my thoughts
on the wings of birds
that carve their way through air,
in slow, certain formation.

Poetry, you go —
go again,
cross the ridges draped
in disciplined greens,
and follow the river,
her silver thread winding,
bending, curving,
twisting in fluid grace.

Place my dreams
upon her dancing waves,
those restless thrill-seekers,
forever flowing, forever young.

And then, poetry, you go —
go again,
cross the worn roads,
and lose yourself,
for a while,
among the trees.

Listen to the winds
murmuring,
whispering,
muttering,
and chattering
with the old leaves.

Place my love
upon the gentle breeze —
the one that drifts inward,
carrying its unseen bliss,
soft as prayer,
wild as light.

Poetry, you go —
and take me with you…

I Can Choose

I can choose to cross the peak,
or wait beneath a quiet hill,
or simply sit where roads bend sharp,
and let the air grow still.

I can choose to paint the sky,
or shape the clouds with drifting hue,
or sketch your thoughts in secret shades—
in strokes that shimmer through.

I can choose to read your mind,
your guesses, dreams, or fears unspoken,
or close the page and walk away,
with every tether broken.

I can choose to walk beside
your words, your silence, or your sigh—
or simply smile with wicked grace,
and pass you, drifting by.

I can choose to cross the river,
or dive into the vast unknown—
or sail beneath your guarded waves,
across your no-go zone.

I can choose to play the muse,
or write the script and steal the scene—
be your riddle, or your ruin,
or neither—just serene.

Until The Night Forgets Itself

The drizzle never hurries.
Nor do I.
We have time—
and silence—
and long, glistening streets
to keep us company
until night forgets itself
and slips away.

Echoes From the Margins

Go, Poetry, Go—
find the pages I lost,
where childhood dreams
lie under frost,
in corners where moonlight
wanders and wanes—
and silence forgets
what still remains.

Bring me the copy
I buried in sighs,
where ink still trembles
with teenage lies—
a crooked stanza,
a stolen phrase,
from wild-eyed nights
and breathless days.

Go, poetry, go—
while the moon leans low,
trace those lines
I used to know—
to the girl next door
with wind in her dress,
black eyes aglow,
a quiet yes.

Give her the verses—
laced in fire,
drenched in dream
and shy desire—
words I wrote
on starlit sheets,
in summer's quiet
and heartbeat beats.

Go, sweetheart, go—
bring back those times
I read alone
in secret rhymes,
when memory burned
and sleep was far,
and every word
still knew her star.

The Song Beneath Silence

– Some songs are only heard by the heart that dares not speak them.

There are ways you touch my heart —
in those moments when
the sky stains itself violet with longing,
when the wine forgets its color and darkens to blue,
when the stars unfasten themselves,
drifting down like murmured confessions.

And in that silence,
what stirs cannot bear a name—
some magic dims
the moment breath gives it shape.

There are ways you stir my buried thoughts —
in those moments when
the past shudders awake,
shaking dust from ancient dreams,
when forgotten pages
turn of their own sorrow.

And what returns
comes barefoot, half-shadow, half-flame—
some memories flinch
at the light of a voice.

There are ways you speak within my mind —
in those moments when
even the birds grow still in their wings,
when clouds tarnish their silver
and whisper strange promises to the wind.
and your silence sings louder than song.

And that song...
it lies curled beneath the quiet,
too fragile for breath,
too sacred for sound—
a note held forever
in the throat of silence.

The First Flame

It wasn't patience
or poetry—
it was the way
your hand brushed mine
like it had always known the route.
The way your eyes
burned through silence
and lit something
I didn't know
was waiting to be touched.
You smiled—
and in that moment,
everything that came after
had already begun.

Let Me Drown in That Moment

Poetry, you go—
find the bird
that sang each morning
outside my window,
through summer light
and soft autumns,
nested in green-shadowed branches,
waking me gently
from dreams I've long forgotten.

Poetry, you go—
gather the shadow
of the old banyan tree,
where we sat for hours,
saying nothing,
saying everything—
pain and bliss
braided in silence
between our fingers.

Poetry, you go—
find the song—
that half-heard refrain,
spilled from a passing radio,
stirring something nameless,
echoing down
the mind's worn halls
like a ghost thought
that never left.

Poetry, you go—
bring back the rain,
its scent rising
from dust and stone—
and the girl
with droplets tracing
her cheeks
as she blinked,
and smiled,
and looked away.

Poetry, you go—
bring the glass
that burned going down.
Bring the fire,
the pen,
the page—
leave the rest.

Just pour me
into that old light—
and let me drown
in the hush
before forgetting.

The Mug On The Left

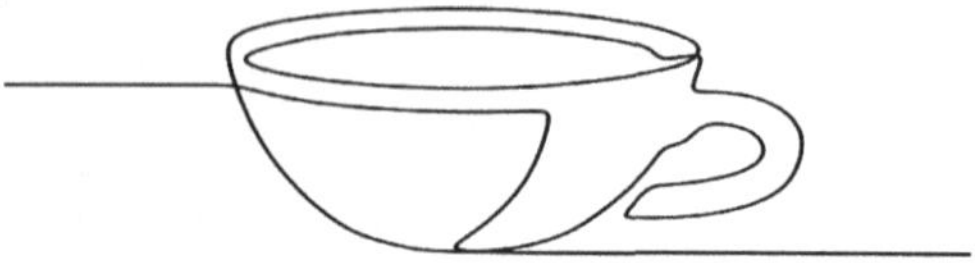

You used to take
the mug on the left—
the chipped one,
with the hairline crack
that never spread.
I offered the newer ones.
You always chose that.

I kept it,
even after the others broke
or disappeared.
Now it sits by the window,
catching morning light
like it still has something to say.

I don't use it.
I don't clean it.
Sometimes, I just watch it—
as if memory could steep.

There's still a strand of your hair
in the spine of that old book
you left behind.
I never marked the page,
but the book always opens there.

Your silence fills the rooms
the way music does
after it stops—
still echoing,
still there.

Sometimes I reply
to messages
you never sent.

And the day you left—
you didn't say a word.
You just left
the mug on the left.

A Moment on The Stairs

As I stood on the failing stairs
I remembered the day you left—
brushed me aside,
stepped out,
the door left ajar.

The steps faded.
The sound echoed
for a while.
Only the scent remained—
one I could fold away,
like a letter,
for days like this
when silence needs a name.

The Green Bangle

You live in my inbox now –
a few lines from long ago.
Some tender,
some teasing,
mostly nothing at all…
unless…
You place a table,
a cappuccino,
and a face
resting on two quiet fists –
blue eyes caught
between auburn streaks of light.
Then it means something..

The green bangle –
the one you left behind last evening –
I still keep it.

Sometimes I spin it between my fingers,
sometimes I lift it to my eyes,
as if to see beyond.
Or maybe –
just to focus
on the music I once played
across your ribs –
before the sun rose,
before the birds remembered to sing.
I saw you once
walking down the street,
your steps trailing nothing in particular.
Maybe you were full of nothingness,
or loneliness –
or maybe… happiness.
I wouldn't know.

Sometimes in my mind,
I still see the window –
you, standing alone,
lost in thought,
one hand brushing back your hair,
the other wrist
wearing that same green bangle.
Maybe it still adorns you.
Maybe it doesn't.
I don't know its fate…
unless, of course,
you choose to tell me...
with a status update.

What Was Left in the Margin

I just want you—
with all you carry:
your silences wrapped in midnight,
your sorrow like wet stone,
the ache that gnaws behind your eyes,
your quiet, unspoken ruins,
those dawn-lit fragments of dreams
no one stayed long enough to hear.

Pleasure—
you may keep.
Bring me the dark.
Come with your empty vessel,
your hollowed grief,
and set sail
on the soft unrest of me.

The Wine Will Know

I will write a few lines—
with raindrops,
along the curved rim of a waiting glass.
You may never trace them,
but the wine will know—
and it will stir a flame
in the quiet corners of your chest
you thought long extinguished.

And then—
I will write a few more lines,
with the last of the rain,
on a folded slip of paper,
soft as breath.
You will not see them.
They are mine alone—
to read alone,
in the pause between moments,
and remember you
as one remembers
a poem that once
held them whole.

And that is enough.

III. Nude and Other Lies

" We bare the skin with ease—
but truth stays dressed in shadows,
whispering promises
between lips that never speak it."

Nudes And Other Lies

She sits in one corner of my room,
that's her usual place,
unless I shift the easel to some other corner
to protect her from curious guests –
the kind who sip their drinks too slowly
and let their glances linger too long.

The ones who drop in unannounced
for a drink maybe or some unfinished work
I promised on some long forgotten lazy afternoon,
between smudged sketches and lazy cigarettes
the kind of promises meant to vanish with the smoke.

She watches me in that still way she always has,
not pleading, but with the quiet ache
of not knowing whether I'll wrap her in shadow,
leave her barely draped, or strip her bare again –
Not with shame, but with brushstrokes
designed to seduce… but again

She knows I don't paint restraint that well
Nakedness is never that simple

I suppose she fears the eyes of others
more than she fears mine —
the way they assess her inch by inch,

with practiced politeness,
coated in lust they pretend to conceal.
They call it critique.

She knows better.
So do I.

At times,
I imagine her waiting - not for fame or form –
but for the buttery warmth of paint smoothing
across her hips, a soft lacquer sealing the story
her skin never got to tell.

Maybe she longs for bold, accented strokes
to lift her curves, which I knew better…
better than the soft bias in her own reflection
and better than those who drank from her excess,
who praised her with baroque words,
then disappeared

leaving fingerprints
only I can still see.

And maybe I delay because

I like her unfinished –
like a breath held…

like heat just before the burn,
like a moan left to echo in an empty room.
like a starlight yet to hit our eyes

She waits.
And I wait.
Not for applause.
Not for completion.
Only for the moment
I can no longer help myself.

What I Told Myself

You could wear a flowing red skirt,
ruby flames swaying from your ears,
your nails lacquered in the colour of fever–
and glide through the city with practiced grace,
catching glances like sparks in passing light–
but all of it would ring hollow,
until my lines gave it breath
and made it burn.

You could roll your jeans, step barefoot
onto wet grass, and spin through the rain,
splashing puddles into the aching air–
your arms outstretched, head thrown back–
you might still stir a few hearts
but the dance would wander, lost and soundless,
until my music folded itself
into your steps.

You could bare that dimple–the one
that eclipses your smile,
the one that could melt a thousand strangers–
and set a crowded café ablaze.
But even that, sweet fire, would smoulder,
waiting, breathless,
until I poured crimson wine into the moment,
raised the glass to my lips,
and drank you whole.

In Measures I Decide

Don't come to me
like a medicine bottle—
labelled and exact,
with sterile lines
and instructions for safe use.
I cannot love
in cautious sips,
prescribed between meals,
measured out in fear.

Don't come to me
like the tide—
rising only
when the moon permits,
retreating on schedule
before the sand gets too warm.
I cannot love
with borrowed gravity,
or borrowed grace.

Come to me
like wine—
ripe and reckless,
brimming to the edge.
Let me take you
by the neck,
tilt you into my mouth,
and drink.
Let me taste
the sweetness,
the fire,
the ruin,
the bloom.
Let it stain.
Let it spill.
Let it burn on the way down.
I will call it love—

in measures I decide.

There are times
I write you into being —
to bend the air around your absence,
to make old mirrors crack with recall,
to haunt the places even you forgot.

And there are times
the page stays bare —
silent as a field
waiting for rain.

And still,
you arrive in the pause
between unwritten lines —
not summoned,
but always returning

A Draught for The Dreamer

Go, poetry, go —
to the keeper of ale,
whisper of longing,
of dreams grown pale.

Ask for a draught
of mint and despair,
and a woman whose laughter
hangs light in the air.

A woman who listens,
whose silence is wise,
whose gaze, when it falls,
wears no thin disguise.

A woman who lingers,
with a chalice of red,
while I summon lost verses
from books never read.

A woman who listens,
whose eyelids grow still
who gathers each tremor
like leaves on a hill.

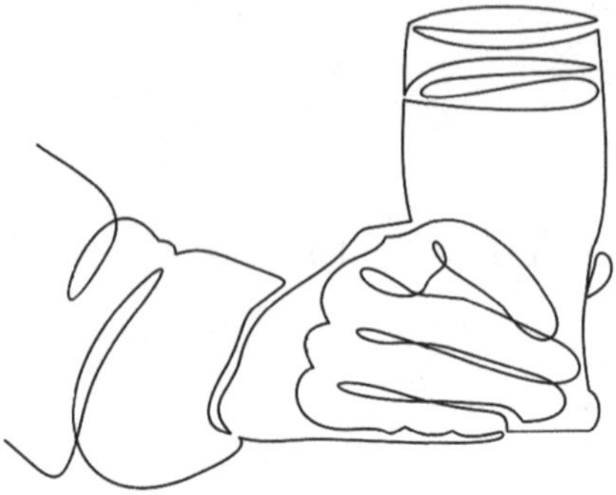

A woman whose beauty
wears spectacles fine,
whose soul rises distant
from the dust of the line.

A woman who cradles
each verse, each refrain,
and hums them back softly
like rain upon rain.

Go, poetry, go —
to the barman of dusk,
and barter my rhymes
for her hand, if you must.

Or tell him I'll wander,
till the end of all seas,
with her name folded softly
like mist in the breeze

Dreams Ancient, Dreams Forbidden

At times...
I wish to be the scarlet sky
that slips into your ocean,
lending it fire,
smiling through your ripples
as you float alone
through elusive dreams—
dreams ancient,
dreams forbidden.

*

At other times...
I long to be the night
that stirs within your sleep,
casting quiet glimmers,
flickering like a candle
as you drift alone
through shadowed thoughts—
thoughts primal,
thoughts forbidden.

*

And again, at times...
I yearn to be the rain
that waits within your silence,
gilding the grass with silver
as you walk alone
through roads forgotten—
roads older than longing,
roads forbidden.

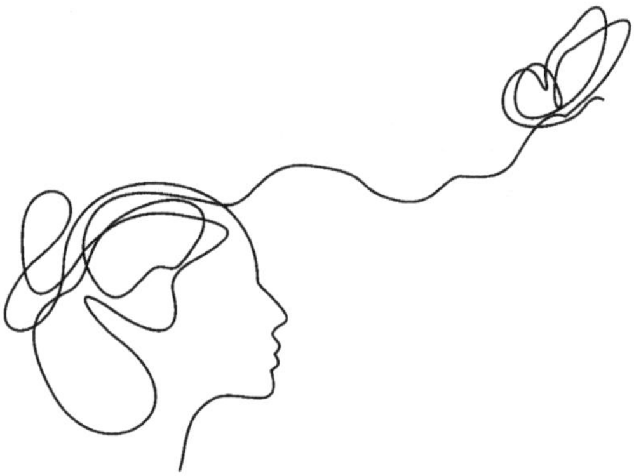

*

And always,
a breath away—
too near to reach,
too far to stay.

Secrets Folded in Silence

You have the right
to assume —
that the poems I stitch together,
the words I coax from stubborn light,
the pictures I half-paint, then abandon,
the colors I spill on careless margins,
the thoughts I transpose from vanished dreams,
the bird that wheels beyond reach,
the river that forgets its name among stones,
the meadow sleeping under heavy gold,
the silence that hums when no one's near,
the stars that wink with old mischief,
the sky that leans too close at dusk —

and all the things
that haunt my crumpled pages:
the apparent,
the abstract,
the nonsense dressed as truth,
the truth disguised as nonsense —
the yearning,
the hunger,
the ache sewn into laughter —

all of it,
and more than all,
are about you.
Only you.

You have the right to assume…
And I —
I'll take the quiet pleasure
of smiling to myself,
like a secret in the dark
that waited
for no one—

I Will Leave a Few Blank Pages

Today,
I will leave
a few blank pages untouched —
to write you some nonsense
maybe
some other day.
I will also gather
a few vintage words,
and tuck them away
to tell you
some other day.

Today,
I will hide
the ripples of feeling
beneath still waters,
to paint them for you
some other day.
I will also bottle
the restless pride
brimming in my chest,
to pour it out
some other day.

Today,
I will gather
a handful of silences,
and leave them waiting
on the threshold of tomorrow.

IV. Ways of Not Arriving

"Not every road leads forward—
some dissolve into silence,
others vanish beneath the weight
of unspoken farewells."

Sometimes, I Just Want to Be the Road

Sometimes...
I just want to be the road—
not the traveler,
not the map,
but the dark ribbon of forgetting
that slips across the earth
with no need for arrival.

The black-silver path
cutting through the spread of green,
where time grows moss
and wheels remember
what feet forgot.

Let me wind through hills
like an old song
no one wrote down—
flutes echoing
from a shepherd's solitude,
disappearing into mist-wrapped folds,
reappearing
with twilight's sigh
and the scent of woodsmoke.

Let a river walk beside me—
a silver braid
carrying moonlight
like old secrets.
We won't speak—
but we'll understand.

Let the stars trail quietly above,
tiny flames
that know my name.
Let dew gather on my edges
like unspoken blessings,
and night curl
around my shoulders
as I pass through forgotten fields
and villages
where voices once lingered
like smoke.

Let me touch
that which has slipped from memory—
a whisper on a weathered surface,
a shadowed way
where echoes linger in the silence,
the stillness that bridges
one age to another.

I long to be that path—
not laid with assurance,
not crafted for charts—
but for awe.

The path murmured softly,
beneath ancient boughs
and twilight's gentle beings.
The path that lingers on,
yet never departs.

The keeper of each stride,
guarding whispers
as if they were sacred,
each silence
a reverent invocation.

Indeed... at times,
I yearn to be the path—
the one unclaimed,
and forever remembered.

To Lose My Way

I set out
not to arrive,
but to lose my way—
to slip through the seams
of well-lit roads,
to vanish into the folds
of what cannot be named.

I had wandered too long
through the order of straight lines,
where meaning hides
in polished certainty.
But the soul—
the soul longs to dissolve
where maps fall silent.

I left behind
the watchful gates of caution,
where once I buried
my trembling wish to fly.
But it kept calling—
in the silence between thoughts,
in the pull of unseen stars.

I moved through the crowd
of familiar faces,
but none of them
knew my name.
So I turned
toward the voice
that echoed from within.

The Shore Where I Lose Myself

-Some journeys end before they begin

If a river
brushed against the edges of your stillness,
I would slip my vessel into its flow,
and drift beside that half-lit shore—
not to reach,
but to remain.
And in the dimming gold of day,
I would anchor breath to your nearness,
and gather time
around the shape of your name.

Should untamed breezes
dance through your untroubled locks,
I would behold the dusk assemble.
each filament a weave
of darkness and light.
In that gentle chaos,
I would discover the form of stillness—
a mystery only twilight
could comprehend.

And if the night
descended upon us
like a whisper unuttered,
I would not pursue it—
only heed,
the vision

I was destined to embrace.

It began like mist —
not near, not far, only there.

And now —
I see you walking,
everywhere:
in day and in night,
through the quiet corridors of thought,
across the blurred fields of dreams,
wandering the veils of memory,
threading through fantasy,
drifting across the quiet of my trance —
and even now,
walking quietly
between the hesitant lines
of these words.

The Way It Was

One might say it's dark in here—
except for sunlight
spilling like slow honey,
casting long shadows
on the wooden floor.

The place is mostly empty now.
Just me,
and a black cat
ghosting between table legs,
hunting for crumbs
or warm memories.

These tables once pulsed—
fingers drumming jazz,
ice in glasses,
words swirling like smoke
caught in lamplight.

Somewhere in the back,
you laughed with your whole mouth.
Your foot found mine—
the quiet language of touch,
between sips and glances.

Now only the faint rings
of old tumblers remain,
etched like ghosts in the wood.
And I trace them,
as if memory could be summoned
by fingertips.

The bottles behind the bar
reflect nothing but the past.
A tune plays—
more memory than music—
and I swear I hear your voice
in the hum of the fan.

Nights come quieter now.
A few old men
sip silence.

Still, I sit
at our table—
the fifth from the door—
waiting for the lights to flicker
and your shadow
to take its place

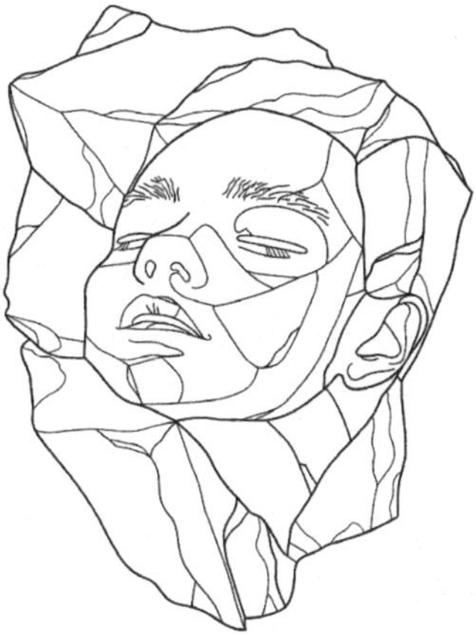

V. Nocturne of the Forgotten

"In the hush between midnight and memory,
the forgotten stir—
not as ghosts,
but as echoes still waiting to be named."

After a Million Years

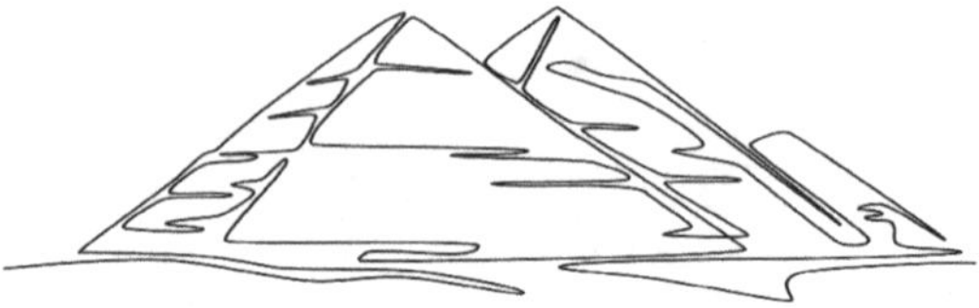

And when—
after a million years,
the last grains of desert wind
settle into silence,
they may find
an anklet,
half-buried where you once danced
beneath a sky
that no longer exists.

Maybe,
a charred patch of earth
where we lit our fire.
A stone, perhaps,
etched with names
now unspoken—
the curves and corners
of a language long lost.

And the flute—
cracked, silent—
still holding
the echo
of the melody I played for you
beneath a night
no instrument remembers.

A scarf, maybe—
faded, wind-softened,
its colors browned by time.
Beads and bangles,
scattered like stardust
beside a dry riverbed
that once knew our footsteps.

They will place them in jars,
tag them,
and display them under lights
like relics
from a world
that must have known beauty.

And they will redefine
civilization.
They will reshape
language,
reimagine
art,
music,
love—
writing theories in the margins
of our dust.

of what they cannot name.

But deep in the stillness of the archives,
beneath glass and codes and numbers,
something will remain—
a breath,
a pulse
uncatalogued.

And there,
where no scholar thinks to look,
will rest
the bones of a sonnet,
still bearing
the shape of love—
unwritten,
but never lost.

Night Without a Moon

-Even the stars have seen too much to speak.

I spent a night in Wadi Rum —
a night without a moon.
The stars spilled like secrets
across a sky untouched by time.
The desert held its breath,
the sand still warm
from the sun's long reign.

The Bedouins brewed tea in the dark.
They did not name the stars —
they already knew them.
Their silence was older than language.

Somewhere west, Petra slept,
carved into the skin of the stone —
facades weathered by wind and war,
where traders once rested
on the spine of empire and incense.
Romans passed here,
left coins, arches, and broken gods.

Beneath my feet:
a thousand trails buried in dust.
Above my head:
not a single star out of place.

How is it,
that the heavens remain unmoved —
while kingdoms fall,
faiths fracture,
and cities forget their names?

The constellations
do not mourn
the collapse of marble.
They witnessed it all —
the rise,
the exile,
the erasure —
and still they gleam,
indifferent and divine.

In the hush between two dunes,
I almost asked their names.
But the Bedouins stirred the embers,
and I kept still —
as if to listen
to something older
than speech.

Through the Dust of Empires

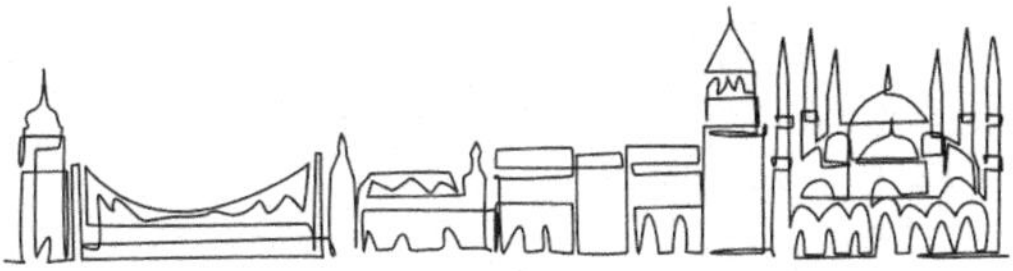

Across centuries, I've wandered—
a lone sojourner from forgotten realms.
This path—I have traced it many times;
even the boatmen of the Bosphorus
must surely know my name.

The plains now sleep beneath soft green,
the thunder of hooves long faded to mist.
Yet still I walk —
and the mute, unmoving mountains
bear witness in their stony silence.

Just beyond the bones of Anastasian stone,
where ivy clings to fractured walls,
if you can read the script time left behind,
you'll find my name — carved, and alone.

This gleaming city sings in restless light,
its towers burn beneath the sun,
but buried beneath that golden weight
another city dreams — undone.

Beneath the banks and marble cafés
lie vaulted halls and silent ground,
walls reduced, and empires folded —
their stories drowned without a sound.

And if the muezzin's cry should wake you
at dawn, when dust begins to rise —
look eastward through the trembling light:
you'll see a shadow stir the skies.

It is I —
returning once more from buried years,
to raise again my citadel
of memory, dreams, stone,
and silent spears.

The Rue of Light and Smoke

They once called it the Rue des Martyrs—
a slope of saints and sinners climbing
toward the white dome of forgiveness.
Painters bled colour onto cobblestones,
and girls with violets in their teeth
sang for coins in the shadow of Sacré-Cœur.

Now they call it Montmartre.

I sit beneath a cracked green awning,
espresso cooling beside a half-smoked cigarette,
watching the dusk unfurl her black silk gloves.

Once, a poet died for a metaphor here,
and no one noticed till the morning.
A dancer fell in love with her own reflection,
and a butcher painted nudes in his cellar
because God never made meat so lovely.

Postcards faded.
Pimps grew polite.
The brothels turned to bistros
serving vegan coq au vin.

The avenue still smoulders —
with velvet dreams and vinegar breath,
with Chanel and secondhand sweat,
with runway heels clicking past
the graffiti of ghosts.

Here, roses cost too much.
Desire is styled and staged.
A girl in Dior and chipped nail polish
blows kisses to a busker
playing Piaf in a hoodie.

The Champs-Élysées gleams nearby,
still polishing its glass smile,
where lovers lean into each other
like questions with no answer.
Perfume laces the air
like soft-spoken lies.

A painter sketches tourists in ten strokes or less,
then lights a cigarette
with the same match he used for his hope.
A drag queen prays before going on stage.
A boy with poems in his coat
asks no one in particular for forgiveness.

And still they come —
the fakers, the seekers, the truly undone —
to this boulevard of illusion and appetite.
They buy more than silk here.
They buy attention.
They buy relevance.
They buy the chance
to walk the same stones
as someone who once meant something.

I swirl the espresso,
bitter and precise,
watching the night strut by
in heels and hunger.

They once called it the Rue des Martyrs.
Now they call it Paris—

and pretend it's always been this beautiful

Skye, Where the Wind Forgets
(Isle of Skye, Scotland)

The Cuillin rise—
sharp-boned and sky-stained,
as if the gods left
their unfinished thoughts
scattered in stone.

Mist slips like memory
through the heather,
cloaking what it chooses,
leaving the rest
to be imagined.

Fishing boats rock
at half-forgotten piers,
tethered like old stories—
their prayers stitched
into salt and rope.

I stood where the road thinned,
where the land gave way to wind.
No one else for miles.
Only the silence
of sheep-dotted hills
and a single raven
riding the air
like a question.

A castle—half bone, half dream—
rose from the cliffs,
watching the water
the way memory watches
what it cannot reclaim.

I sat on a stone,
warmed by nothing,
and let the world pass
through me—
not touching,
but echoing.

Skye does not speak.
It listens.
And in its wind-chiseled silence,
I began to forget
what I once thought
I had to hold.
And in forgetting,
I remembered less.

The Long Acre

— seen from a diner window

They once called it the Long Acre —
a stretch of grit between past and promise,
where carriage wheels bit into cobblestone,
and lanterns leaned into rain like old men.

Now they call it Times Square.

I sit behind a fogged-up window,
coffee cooling in a chipped white cup,
watching the night dress itself in voices.

A woman once danced on a rooftop in red,
while jazz spilled from a basement bar,
and two boys kissed in an alley
before being swallowed by the dark.

Posters dreamed
and shed their skin.
Flags forgot
who held them last.
Tongues tangled
in smoke and glass.
The drums—
they remembered nothing.

The avenue is a restless mural —
every shade of skin,
every shape of prayer,
every kind of hunger.

Here, saris sway beside sequins,
turmeric blends with bourbon,
and perfume flirts with gutter steam.
Shawarma, gospel, glitter, grief —
all braided beneath a blinking sky.

Now neon crowns every corner.
Screens flicker like restless gods.
There are dancers in gold,
merchants of glass,
puppets, prophets,
and a man selling poems
for ten dollars a line.

A violin weeps beneath a scaffold.
Laughter falls from a fire escape.
Somewhere, behind a deli,
a mural waits in silence.
Somewhere, above it all,
a woman still dances in red.

And still they come —
the dreamers, the lost, the radiant and raw —
poured like wine into the veins of this street.
They sell more than wares here.
They sell wonder.
They sell forgetting.
They sell the feeling
of being part of something
too big to name.

I stir my cup,
watching the stream go by,
a pilgrim to the shrine of light and noise.

They once called it the Long Acre.

Now they call it Times Square.

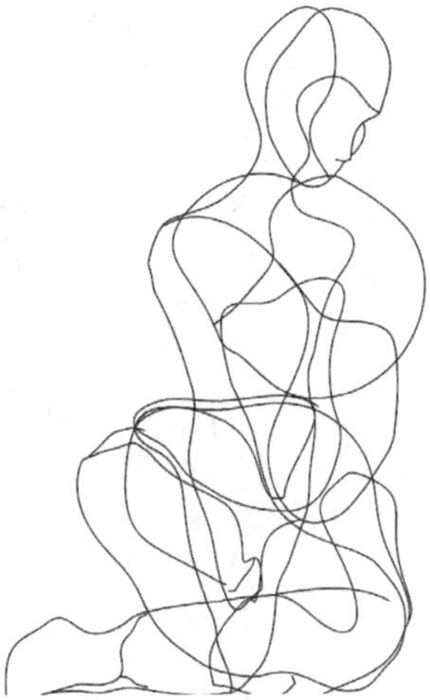

VI. Interlude Before the Epilogue

"Not yet the end,
but the breath that lingers
before silence decides
what must be remembered."

And No One Will Know

No one will know
that we walked this earth,
that the dust clung to our feet
as we wandered through forgotten streets,
that the wind once whispered our names
through alleyways of time.

No one will know
that we sat by the glass-paned door
of an old coffee shop,
where steam rose from porcelain cups
and the air smelled of rain and stories,
that we watched a tram rattle past,
carrying strangers wrapped in yesterday's thoughts.

No one will know
that our laughter brushed against old walls,
that our hands traced the chipped paint
of doors now sealed in silence,
that once, in the murmur of dusk,
we sat by the river,
where the quiet waters held our reflections
and never let go.

No one will know
that the autumn leaves crunched beneath our steps,
that we lingered under the flickering street lamps,
that the yellow cabs rushed past
while we stood still,
counting moments like fallen petals
on a street that had no name.

No one will know
that we ran across fields of gold,
that the wild grass kept our footprints
until the wind swept them away,
that we carved verses
into the bark of ancient trees
believing poetry could live forever.

No one will know
that we watched the tide come and go,
that the sea sang to us in a language
lost to time,
that once, atop an unnamed hill,
we sat beneath a silent moon
with nothing but the sky between us.

No one will know
that the rain kissed our faces
on nights when the world slept,
that the scent of jasmine
clung to your hair,
that I hummed a melody
no instrument has ever played.

No one will know
that we stood at the edge of time,
waiting, waiting,
before footsteps followed...
until history erased us
and memory turned to dust.
And yet, somewhere,
a piece of scarf,
a note in an old book,
a sigh in the wind,
a forgotten receipt from an old café,
a painting, half-finished,
its colors fading like a memory,
will whisper

we were...

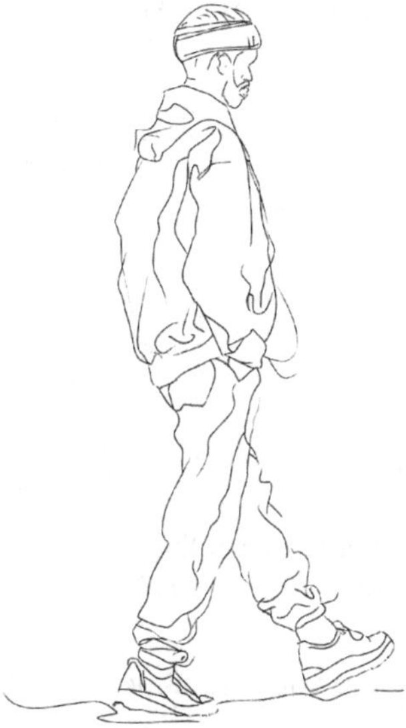

VII. Before the Light Returns

"Before the light returns,
time thins to a hush—
and in that waning pause,
the self, long scattered, gathers
into a final knowing."

The Road That Beckons

It begins where silence breaks
into a curve—
a winding road, veined with light,
where sky leans in
to brush the hills
and vanishes before you can name it.

Here, clouds descend like questions,
drifting low into the ravine,
not to shroud
but to reveal—
the ache in the valley's breast,
the memory of rain.

Pines rise like ancient monks
each needle holding the story
of a thousand winters.
And somewhere, a barbet calls—
not for reply
but to remember its voice.

Mist drapes itself
over the shoulder of the waterfall
woven from sky-water and light.
It does not fall.
It surrenders.

The river below—
turquoise and trembling—
knows how to kiss the stone
without breaking it.
She knows the way
without asking.

And me—
I am neither sky
nor stone…

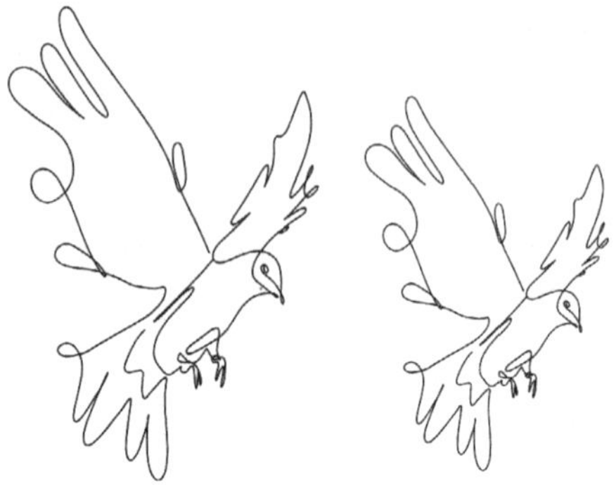

In the Quiet of Dusk

In the hush of twilight,
as the heavens shed their hues,
and weary wings falter,
lost in the vastness—
I remain still
under a canopy
that has silenced its whispers.

Amidst the weaving branches
and the whispering breeze,
a secret melody floats by—
not loud,
but with intent,
as though it bears a whisper
too delicate for the daylight to grasp.

Beyond the hills,
in the land of wandering clouds,
evening blushes
with the sigh of distant longing.
The light there
is not gold,
but the memory of gold.

The forest sighs
in trembling leaves,
and the wind leaves behind
a flute-song,
unfinished—
as though someone, somewhere,
forgot to stop dreaming.

In the mystery of this hour,
a beauty unnamed
sings before my voice arrives.
Some notes are not born of sound—
but wait,
just beneath the breath,
where dreams gather
and sometimes dissolve.

Some dreams unfurl.
Others simply scent the dusk.
But their fragrance lingers
in the corner of your gaze—
a silence that glows
before the stars arrive.

What I Wore

I kept waiting—
like a night bird
on the high branch
of a lonely oak,
watching,
waiting for you
to spread your wings.
I stayed locked
with the night,
with the stars
blinking
from behind
a million light years.
I stayed fixed
like the mountains—
ancient wisdom
filling my senses.
I wore your silence
like a borrowed coat.
And then one day,
it no longer fit.

Before the Edges Blurred

Sometimes,
when the rain falls hard—
drumming its wild heart on the trembling leaves,
chanting the rhythm of longing
from the roots hidden deep in earth's soul—
and when the scent of soil
rises like memory,
cradling me in an ancient silence…
I long to lie down
on the wet green grass,
arms outstretched,
eyes closed—
to see the rain.

Sometimes,
when clouds drift away with longing,
wearing their sorrow in shades of grey,
chanting the music of the deep blue
and when old, forgotten thoughts
return in soft shrouds—
gathering like mist on the windows of my dreams…
I wish to rest
on fallen leaves,
arms open wide,
eyes closed—
to see the cloud
as it weeps above me.

And sometimes,
when the wind arrives unannounced,
a quiet traveler from nowhere,
carrying the breath of places
I have never been
but somehow remember—
It touches me softly, like a whisper long forgotten
too quiet for language
Then, I lie beneath a restless sky,
arms lifted to the breeze,
eyes closed not in sleep,
but in wonder—
to feel the wind
and remember who I was…

When Night Wears the Face of Light

There comes a time—
not marked by clocks,
nor measured in hours—
when silence deepens
into something more ancient
than sleep.

Not darkness,
but a gathering of shadows
yearning to transform into stars.
What title shall I bestow upon this silence—
this ethereal instant
caught between oblivion and fire?

The sun lingers,
casting shadows
that stretch and sway.
It withdraws,
tucking itself into the fabric of the heavens
like a soft-spoken spell
that only the darkness can decipher.

As I traverse this waning path,
not in sorrow,
but in an elusive
and hallowed awareness:
that which has slipped away
is at times not truly absent,
merely reshaped into a form
too delicate for the sun's embrace.

I do not mourn.
I do not pray.
I listen.

A single note
drifts through the air—
not sung,
but remembered
by the bones of the earth.

Perhaps it is joy
that has no language,
or sorrow
that has outgrown its name.

The past wears no face here—
only fragrance.
A trace of warmth
in a place I don't recall visiting.
A softness
at the edge of thought.

And still I move forward—
not toward morning,
but through it—
through the veil
where time loosens its grip,
and light
forgets it was ever afraid
of the dark.

Yes—
this is where the night begins to bloom,
where stillness becomes seed,
and the self unfolds
quietly
like a flame without fire.

And if I vanish here,
let it be without echo.
Let it be like the first breath of dawn—
not announced,
but altering the world
with nothing more
than presence.

This Is the Hour When Silence Breathes

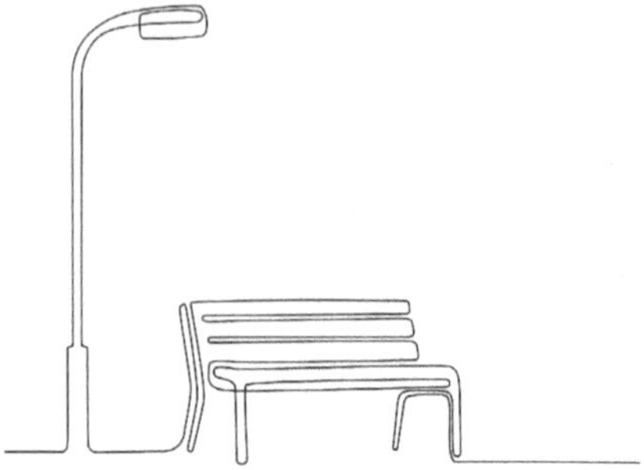

Now the night is silent –
and silence,
with darkness curled around its fingers,
spreads like a quiet empire.
Stil, somewhere,
bubbles rise—
small sounds
surfacing
on forgotten streets.
They drift
through alleys and footpaths,
curling into cracks,
nestling in corners—
in pores,
in roots,
in veins and ribs and whispered breath.

The lamppost stands—
tall, blind,
casting light on others
but never seeing
its own reflection
beneath a thousand passing feet.

Not all sounds
are meant to be heard.
Some hide
behind the bustle of rain.
Some curl
into the folds of grief,
or dissolve
in silent defiance.
A few flicker
in the sheen of tired eyes.
A few remain unnamed,
circling like ghosts
in the hush before dawn.
And now,
in this midnight hour,
the echoes of those scattered words
will stay –
not lost,
just resting quietly
in the pages of my notebook.

Someone Calls Me

Someone calls me -
a breath folded in morning light,
a murmur stitched from dawn,
a fragment of a dream,
luring me to the edge of the unseen,
where the clouds blush in slow surrender,
and silence leans in like a lover
with stories too soft for language.

Somewhere above,
a bird breaks free of its shadow,
wings carving through wind without hesitation.
It does not look back.
Neither will I.

There is no chart,
only the call of a waiting horizon,
the shimmer of a dream not mine yet,
a future I've never named
but somehow recognize.

Let earth remain behind,
with its familiar walls and gentle names.
I carry no sorrow—only stillness.
No destination—only direction.
No fear—only the wind.

And if I am forgotten
in the slow turning of seasons,
know that I was never gone,
just scattered in silence
like moonlight folding into tide,
or wind becoming voice in a distant forest.

Somewhere,
beneath a sky that remembers,
she will walk—
not knowing the path carries my name.
She may pause
beneath a tree where I once rested,
or hum the tune the wind once taught me,
and not know why it feels like home.

And that will be enough.

And So, My Lines Go On

I. Farewell

My lines now float
across the open sky—
clouds whispering
it's time to say goodbye.
To leave it all behind
and take the winding way,
through mist and silence,
through the fog of grey.

A shepherd's flute
calls from distant hills,
the moon hides low
as the meadow stills.
These lines arrive
like dawn's first light,
a promise rising
on the edge of night

II. The Weight

No longer playful,
nor sweet with rhyme—
they carry earth,
the weight of time.
Of nameless faces,
toil and tears,
of silent cries,
and shadowed years.

Of broken men
in endless lines,
of chains and cells,
of unseen crimes.
Of wolves that howl
in hungered lust,
of voices lost
in blood and dust.
They trace the footprints
we try to forget—
through war and loss,
through deep regret.

III. Beyond

Yet still, they flow—
to childhood days,
to rain-washed streets,
to sunlight haze.
The promenade,
the ocean's sound,
those quiet bends
where dreams were found.

They ride the waves—
restless, bold—
breaking on rocks
with stories untold.
Misting the skies
where seagulls cry,
pointing always
where horizons lie.

And I shall go
beyond these seas,
to lands that whisper
with ancient trees.
Barefoot on dew,
in morning light,
with flowers burning
in crimson bright.
To sleep at last
beneath the sky,
arms outstretched—
and let the clouds drift by.

Epilogue

"Not all silences are empty.
Some carry the shape of words
we were never brave enough to speak."

What I Meant to Say

What I meant to say
curled like smoke
in the space between our silences—
it hovered,
a moth brushing the edges of lamplight,
never quite brave enough
to burn.

What I meant to say
left the room
wrapped in the rustle of your leaving,
a shadow tucked into your sleeve,
a name I folded
into the seam of goodbye.

It sat beside you
when the sky turned to glass,
when rain stitched
the windows with forgetting,
when the teacups trembled
from words we didn't spill.

It pressed its breath
into envelopes I never sent,
grew brittle
in the drawers of almosts and maybes.
By the time I turned back,
you were already mist—
and the paper had paled
to dust.

What I meant to say
still leans against the doorframe,
waiting for your eyes
to open that last unfinished page
where silence
had scrawled your name
in ash.

The sky ends here.
But the earth speaks still.

The journey continues—
next, I will write
of people, of struggle,
of war and what it leaves behind.

And if You're Still Listening…

If these poems found you in a quiet moment, thank you for letting them in.

This collection began as a conversation with silence. It waited, like I did, for someone who might listen with the same stillness.

If something here reminded you of a feeling you hadn't named, or a memory you thought you'd forgotten—then the words have done their part.

No praise is necessary. No reviews are asked for. Just this: may you carry a little more quiet with you, and hear yourself more clearly in it.

—Debashis

9 789334 326468

Printed at Repro India Ltd.